Writing a Critical Essay

The Complete Introductory Guide to Writing a Critical Essay for Beginner Students

Book Description

The ability to write a critical essay is an essential skill for every student to learn. Learning how to write the critical essay begins in secondary education, but it doesn't stop there. The critical essay is a specific style of essay that analyzes and interprets the author's purpose, intent, theme, or thesis of a specific body of work. Learning how to write a proper critical essay is crucial for being able to enhance, practice, and apply critical thinking skills.

This book will teach students and learners of any age how to write a critical essay. It will take an introductory approach and assume that the reader has never written a critical essay before. This book will teach students:

- What a critical essay is
- The basic structure to a critical essay
- How to organize a critical essay
- How to write a critical essay

While a person or student may excel at critical thinking skills, it can be difficult to organize those thoughts into a coherent essay that clearly communicates the writer's ideas and interpretations of the text. Learn the basics and transform your writing into proficient communication and analysis.

Melissa Koons

Copyright © 2018 Write Illusion LLC
All rights reserved.
ISBN: 978-1-981828-12-8

Table of Contents

Introduction	**1**
Analysis: Analyze What?	**5**
Brainstorm: It's Raining Ideas!	**41**
Outline: Line it up!	**53**
Write Time, Write Place	**79**
Example Essay	**83**
Conclusion	**107**

Melissa Koons

Introduction

Critical thinking skills are practiced early on in educational programs, and are continuously developed with practice and rigor throughout secondary and post-secondary schooling. Critical thinking is the ability to review the information that is presented to a person and analyze it to form a judgement or assessment. Critical thinking skills are important because they are the skills that will be used to evaluate any information, situation, or project that a person is engaged in—both inside and outside of an educational setting.

These skills are not limited to only scholastic situations. Critical thinking skills are used daily by both young people and adults.
- When looking for a job, you use critical thinking skills to analyze if the position will offer the appropriate number of hours, wages, benefits, and a reasonable commuting distance.
- When being assigned a presentation at work, you will use critical thinking skills to process the requirements and expectations of the presentation so that you can deliver that information to your superior's satisfaction.
- When you are trying to find a friend's house for the first time, or are commuting to a place you've been a hundred times, you will use critical thinking skills to process which route to take to avoid traffic, construction, and back-tracking.
- When meeting someone new, you will use critical thinking skills to evaluate their interests, personality

traits, and character to form an opinion of them and determine the type of relationship (or lack of one) you will have with that person.
- When reading or watching the news, you will use critical thinking skills to evaluate situations and determine your future actions such as: who you will vote for, what locations to avoid, safe practices to adopt, and interesting events to pay attention to.

Critical thinking skills are used daily by everyone. The above are only a few examples of when we apply these skills, but any time we have to assess a situation and make a judgement we are using critical thinking.

Critical thinking skills are taught and strengthened through reading and writing. When reading an essay, story, or article, you are being presented with information. This information is a means to express the author's purpose or intent for writing what they wrote, the theme or major idea that the author wants the reader to walk away with, or the thesis or claim that the author is setting out to prove. The reader will use their critical thinking skills and develop an analysis based on what they interpret the meaning of the text is; the essay, then, is the explanation and defense of this analysis.

Writing a critical essay not only serves to improve the student's understanding of the text at hand and their ability to process information, but also their communication skills. The ability to write a critical essay strengthens and enhances their ability to translate those critical thoughts and analysis into a coherent assessment. Being able to think critically and being able to communicate it effectively, are two different skills.

Introduction

Good communication occurs when a person is able to organize their thoughts, support them with evidence, and provide an explanation to make their point. Not only that, but great communication takes place when people are able to listen, analyze, interpret, and form a judgement based on what someone else presents to them.

This is the exact foundation of a critical essay.

The act of writing gives the writer the opportunity to organize their thoughts and evidence before presenting it. Once a student has been able to grasp the skills and write about it in a coherent critical essay, then they can begin to transfer those skills to other forms of communication including but not limited to: talking, texting, emailing, interviewing, and presenting.

To help students and learners of any age develop these skills, this book will cover the process for writing a critical essay:

- Analysis
- Brainstorming
- Outlining
- Writing

Luckily, there is a formula to constructing a critical essay. Learning this formula and process will strengthen not only your ability to write a critical essay, but your ability to think critically and to communicate.

Melissa Koons

Chapter 1 – Analyze, What?

It can be tempting to skip the planning and brainstorming steps and get right down to writing the essay, but this would be a mistake. Just as the author is writing their text with a clear purpose and direction, your analysis of it needs to have equal focus.

Before you can start writing anything, it is important to first identify your own purpose and what you are wanting to prove with your essay. The basis of a critical essay is defending an analysis that you provide and support with evidence from the text; if you aren't sure what you are looking for in the text, you cannot communicate that defense.

What is an analysis?

An analysis is a detailed look at a topic, subject, or concept. It is the process of examining the elements of structure for interpretation.

With a critical essay, you are typically analyzing the structure of one of three elements:

1. the author's purpose (or intent)
2. the theme
3. the thesis

An analysis is not based on a "right" or "wrong" answer. The basis of an analysis is to be able to evaluate the elements in the text and make a provable claim about them. The way you prove your claim is through evidence found in the text.

Let's Practice:

Below is a poem by Robert Frost. Provide an analysis of the final line:

"Nothing Gold Can Stay" by Robert Frost

Nature's first green is gold,
Her hardest hue to hold.
Her early leaf's a flower;
But only so an hour.
Then leaf subsides to leaf.
So Eden sank to grief,
So dawn goes down to day.
Nothing gold can stay.

Before answering the prompt directly, you need to break down the poem in order to pull out the details and provide an analysis.

What is the poem about? Provide a summary.

_____

_____

_____

_____

_____

_____

Analysis: Analyze, What?

What else could the speaker be talking about other than the seasons: spring turning to winter?

Based on the other possibilities of what you think the speaker may be referring to, what could the last line mean?

The summary of events is what the text is about, but the analysis is what the text is ABOUT.

The big ABOUT is the deeper interpretations and ideas that are being expressed in the text. It is the big ABOUT that you will use as a basis for your claim and the rest of your essay.

What is a claim?

A claim is the point or analysis that you are making based on your interpretation of the text. This is the point you are trying to prove in your essay.

While you can develop an analysis over the entire text, your claim will be focusing on a single point. This gives your essay a singular focus so that you are not presenting too many ideas in one essay. When you have too many ideas in an essay, many of them end up being underdeveloped or not explained at all, which weakens your analysis and critical essay as a whole. It is best to pick one idea from your analysis for your claim and stick to it. This makes it easier for you to develop, support, and explain your claim in the span of a single essay.

When you write your essay, this claim/point will be translated into a thesis statement.

Your essay will have one main claim, or thesis, that you are making throughout the entire paper. Additionally, each body paragraph will also have a claim. These body paragraph claims are the main ideas of each paragraph. They are the specific details that you are proving to support your bigger claim (thesis.)

Your claim, or thesis, can't be anything you want it

to be: it has to be supported by evidence in the text. This means you have to find quotations where the author uses their own words to support the claim you are making. If you cannot find evidence in the text to support your claim, then that claim will not work for a critical essay.

While your claim can't be anything you want it to be, that does not mean there is only one "right" answer. As long as you can find quotations and evidence in the text to support it, you have any number of possible claims that you can make based on your analysis and interpretation of the information.

For some students, it can be overwhelming that there is no one "right" answer. Instead, there are multiple possibilities. The possibility of there being more than one "right" answer is difficult to grasp, and they are concerned with getting it wrong. This concern leads to overthinking and becoming overwhelmed, which makes it nearly impossible for the student to proceed with their essay.

The only way to get a definitive "right" answer for a critical essay is to interview the author and ask them what their intent, theme, or thesis is. Since it is very unlikely that this will happen, it is safe to assume that if you can find enough textual support and evidence to prove your claim, then you're "right."

Instead of becoming overwhelmed, there are several different mindsets that can help:
- Think of it like a scavenger hunt. You have an idea, and are looking for clues in the text to prove your idea is possible.
- Think of it as a challenge. What idea can you come up with and prove with the text?
- Get creative. Ask yourself: how can I look at this information in a way that is new and different?

For example, consider this stanza from "A Poet" by Thomas Hardy:

"For loud acclaim he does not care/ By august or rich or fair,/ Nor for smart pilgrims from afar,/ Curious on where his hauntings are."

Analysis: A poet doesn't care about acclaim for their art by either the rich or scholars. They don't care what people who read it are guessing their meanings and motivations for writing the poems are.

Claim: <u>The poet does not care how their work is received.</u>

Let's Practice:

Looking at the same poem by Robert Frost, come up with three different claims based on your analysis of the final line.

Remember: there are multiple possibilities and analyses that can be made. There is no one right answer. You just have to find evidence in the text to support your idea.

"Nothing Gold Can Stay" by Robert Frost

Nature's first green is gold,
Her hardest hue to hold.
Her early leaf's a flower;
But only so an hour.
Then leaf subsides to leaf.
So Eden sank to grief,
So dawn goes down to day.
Nothing gold can stay.

Your claim should be based on your closer analysis of what else the speaker could be talking about, and what the last line of the poem, "nothing gold can stay," means.

To get you started, here is an example of a claim.

Claim: <u>The last line refers to death.</u>

Using the example above and your own analysis, develop three possible claims. The intent is that you will be able to explain this claim and show where you got your idea from the information in the text.

Analysis: Analyze, What?

Claim 1:

_____

_____

_____

_____

Claim 2:

_____

_____

_____

_____

Claim 3:

_____

_____

_____

_____

Now that you have three claims to choose from, you can begin processing which one you will be able to construct an essay around.

The point of a critical essay is not to be 100% right, it is to think critically and support your analysis with evidence from the text. If you can support your claim with evidence from the text and explain how that evidence supports your claim, then that's all that matters for this essay.

The key to a successful critical analysis and critical essay is textual evidence.

What is textual evidence?

Textual evidence is specific passages, quotations, or details within the text that support the claim you are making.

Textual evidence is the data that you will use to prove your claim. It is the specific lines or quotations from the text that allowed you to make your analysis. These are the details that you used to form your big ABOUT. This is the data that shows where your ideas came from.

For example, consider this stanza from "A Poet" by Thomas Hardy:

"For loud acclaim he does not care/ By august or rich or fair,/ Nor for smart pilgrims from afar,/ Curious on where his hauntings are."

Analysis: A poet doesn't care about acclaim for their art by either the rich or scholars. They don't care what people who read it are guessing their meanings and motivations for writing the poems are.

Claim: The poet does not care how their work is received.

Textual evidence: "For loud acclaim he does not care" and "nor for smart pilgrims from afar"

The textual evidence that supports the claim "the poet does not care how their work is received," is supported by those two lines in the stanza quoted above.

Let's Practice:

Take one of your three claims that you made. Locate three lines or details in the text that support or prove your claim.

"Nothing Gold Can Stay" by Robert Frost

Nature's first green is gold,
Her hardest hue to hold.
Her early leaf's a flower;
But only so an hour.
Then leaf subsides to leaf.
So Eden sank to grief,
So dawn goes down to day.
Nothing gold can stay.

Claim 1:

_____

_____

_____

_____

Textual Evidence 1:

_____

_____

Textual Evidence 2:

Textual Evidence 3:

If you were unable to find three lines or details in the poem to support or prove your claim, then you probably don't have a strong enough foundation for that claim to write a critical essay. Pick another claim and try to locate details in the text that will support it.

This is a common problem that you will encounter when starting an essay. It's okay if your first claim and idea doesn't have enough textual support, that's why you make sure you locate all your textual evidence prior to writing the essay so you can change direction if needed.

Claim 2:

_____

_____

_____

_____

Textual Evidence 1:

_____

_____

_____

_____

_____

Textual Evidence 2:

_____

_____

_____

_____

_____

Textual Evidence 3:

_____

_____

_____

_____

_____

Repeat as necessary until you find three supporting details for your claim. Since you developed three claims in the earlier exercise, try to find three pieces of textual evidence for all three claims that you wrote.

Claim 3:

Textual Evidence 1:

Textual Evidence 2:

Textual Evidence 3:

_____

_____

_____

_____

_____

Textual evidence is vital for proving the writer's claim, but the analysis can't end with that. The writer has to explain how the textual evidence supports the claim. The writer should never assume that the reader will immediately make the connection that the writer wants them to make between the evidence and the claim.

What is the explanation?

The explanation is the development of the idea and how the textual evidence supports the claim that you are making.

For a critical analysis and critical essay you have to explain your reasoning behind your claim and the evidence you chose to support that claim. You already used critical thinking skills to analyze the text and create a claim; now, you have to use those skills again to interpret the information you presented in the evidence and construct a judgement based on that information that supports your claim. This is where you explain how the specific quotations from the text gave you your ideas that you turned into an analysis and then developed into a claim for your essay.

For example, consider this stanza from "A Poet" by Thomas Hardy:

"For loud acclaim he does not care/ By august or rich or fair,/ Nor for smart pilgrims from afar,/ Curious on where his hauntings are."

Analysis: A poet doesn't care about acclaim for their art by either the rich or scholars. They don't care what people who read it are guessing their meanings and motivations for writing the poems are.

Claim: <u>The poet does not care how their work is received.</u>

Textual evidence: "For loud acclaim he does not care" and "nor for smart pilgrims from afar"

Explanation: "For loud acclaim he does not care" shows that the poets does not care how their work is received because it is implied that they are not writing it for acclaim or approval by those who read it. "Nor for smart pilgrims from afar/ Curious on where his hauntings are" proves that the poet does not care how their work is received because they aren't looking for far off scholars to read it and analyze it. The poet does not want to hear other people's opinions and interpretations of their work.

Explaining how the evidence supports the claim is the development of the idea and where critical thinking skills are applied. This is where the writer explains and details their analysis on the author's purpose, the theme, or the thesis.

Let's Practice:

Using the claim (or one of the claims) that you were able to find three details or lines in the text to support, apply critical thinking skills and provide an explanation on how those details support your claim and prove your idea.

"Nothing Gold Can Stay" by Robert Frost

Nature's first green is gold,
Her hardest hue to hold.
Her early leaf's a flower;
But only so an hour.
Then leaf subsides to leaf.
So Eden sank to grief,
So dawn goes down to day.
Nothing gold can stay.

For this practice, you only need to select one of the lines or details from the text that supports your claim to provide an explanation for. In the actual essay, you will do it for each piece of textual evidence that you have.

Claim:

_____

_____

_____

_____

Analysis: Analyze, What?
Textual Evidence:

Explanation:

Author's Purpose or Intent:

When you are asked to identify the author's purpose or intent, you are being asked to figure out why the author wrote the article, essay, or story you read.

Some good questions to ask yourself to figure this out are:
- What is their purpose or motivation for writing what they wrote?
- Why did they bother to sit down and take the time to write this?
- What idea, feeling, or conviction do they want the reader to walk away with after reading this?

Answering these questions will help you identify the author's purpose or intent. Once you have identified the author's purpose, then you can begin to think critically about it. Some critical thinking questions to ask yourself are:
- Did the author effectively communicate their purpose? How? Where?
- What point are they trying to make? Could they have made it better?

When it comes to a critical essay, your opinion on whether or not you agree with the author's purpose is irrelevant: it doesn't matter. Your focus is to analyze the information presented to you objectively and to determine: what is the information, how was it presented, and why was it presented. Your personal opinion is not featured in this type of essay.

Let's Practice:

Using the poem "Nothing Gold Can Stay," answer the critical thinking questions and identify the author's purpose. Read through the poem and then answer the questions below. After you have answered the critical thinking questions, make your claim toward what the author's purpose or intent is.

"Nothing Gold Can Stay" by Robert Frost

Nature's first green is gold,
Her hardest hue to hold.
Her early leaf's a flower;
But only so an hour.
Then leaf subsides to leaf.
So Eden sank to grief,
So dawn goes down to day.
Nothing gold can stay.

1. What is Robert Frost's motivation for writing this poem?

_____

_____

_____

_____

_____

_____

2. Why did he sit down and take the time to write this poem?

3. What idea, feeling, or conviction did he want the reader to walk away with after reading the poem?

Analyze, What?

4. Did the author effectively communicate their purpose?

5. What point was he trying to make? Could it have been clearer?

Now that you have answered these critical thinking questions: identify what the author's purpose is.

Author's Purpose:

Theme:

The theme is the major idea or topic that the author wants the reader to walk away with. A good way to find the theme is to ask:
- What is this story about? (The summary of the major events and/or points in the text.)
- What is this story ABOUT? (This big "ABOUT" is the major idea that the author is presenting and using those major events in the whole text to explain or represent.)
- What am I supposed to learn from this?

The theme can sometimes be simplified into the moral or lesson that the reader should come away with.

It is important to note that the theme is NOT the same as the main idea. A text can have more than one main idea, but it should only have one theme. (There can also be multiple sub-themes, but there will be only one main theme.)

The difference between a theme and a main idea is: the theme is the main topic throughout the entirety of the text, the main idea is the point of each paragraph or section.

Let's Practice:

Using the poem "Nothing Gold Can Stay," answer these critical thinking questions to identify the theme of the poem.

"Nothing Gold Can Stay" by Robert Frost

Nature's first green is gold,
Her hardest hue to hold.
Her early leaf's a flower;
But only so an hour.
Then leaf subsides to leaf.
So Eden sank to grief,
So dawn goes down to day.
Nothing gold can stay.

1. What is the poem about? (Summarize.)

_____

_____

_____

_____

_____

_____

_____

Analyze, What?

2. What is the major idea or moral presented throughout the whole poem?

_____

_____

_____

_____

_____

_____

3. What was the reader supposed to learn from this poem?

_____

_____

_____

_____

_____

_____

Based on your answers to the critical thinking questions above, identify what the theme of the poem is.

Theme:

Thesis:

A thesis is the claim or idea that the author is setting out to prove or defend. Articles, essays, and other forms of non-fiction will have a thesis. Even the critical essay you write will have a thesis statement.

Unlike the author's purpose, the thesis will be stated outright in the non-fiction text. In the case of a thesis, there will only be one possible answer. The thesis is the foundation for the entire non-fiction text, so it should be obvious.

The thesis will be given toward the beginning of the text—usually within the introduction or first body paragraph. This is because the author or writer will want to establish their purpose, and the point they will be making, early on.

The thesis is the author's stance on a particular subject. A good way to find the thesis is to ask:

- What are they wanting to prove?
- Why do they think I should care about what they are writing?

Asking yourself these questions while you read will help you identify the thesis.

Melissa Koons

Let's Practice:

Read this excerpt from Edgar Allan Poe's essay: "The Philosophy of Composition," and answer the critical thinking questions.

"The Philosophy of Composition" by Edgar Allan Poe

Charles Dickens, in a note now lying before me, alluding to an examination I once made of the mechanism of "Barnaby Rudge," says, "By the way, are you aware that Godwin wrote his 'Caleb Williams' backwards? He first involved his hero in a web of difficulties, forming the second volume, and then, for the first, cast about him for some mode of accounting for what had been done."

I cannot think this the precise mode of procedure on the part of Godwin, and indeed what he himself acknowledges, is not altogether in accordance with Mr. Dickens' idea, but the author of "Caleb William" was too good an artist not to perceive the advantage derivable from at least a somewhat similar process. Nothing is more clear than that every plot, worth the name, must be elaborated to its dénouement before any thing be attempted with the pen. It is only with the dénouement constantly in view that we can give a plot its indispensable air of consequence, or causation, by making the incidents, and especially the tone at all points, tend to the development of the intention."

Now that you have read the passage, answer the critical thinking questions below and then identify the author's thesis.

Analyze, What?

1. What is the author wanting to prove?

2. Why do they think you should care about what they are writing?

Author's Thesis:

Analyze, What?

If you are ever unsure as to whether or not you have identified a plausible author's purpose, theme, or thesis there is a way to double check yourself. This method of double checking will make sure that there is a foundation for your idea and that your idea/claim actually relates to the body of work that you are analyzing.

To double check that you have identified a provable purpose, theme, or thesis, read through the text again and look for textual evidence to support the thesis that you came up with.

Follow the rule of three: if you are unable to find at least three pieces of textual evidence to support your claim, then you need to find another claim.

The reason for three pieces of textual evidence is because that implies that the claim is prevalent, or featured continuously, throughout the text. If you can only find two or less, then it might be a main idea or topic in the text, but is not supported enough to be the purpose/theme/thesis.

Now that you have identified what you are looking for and analyzed the text, you can start working on the next step: a brainstorm.

Chapter 2 – It's Raining Ideas!

Brainstorming is the step most commonly skipped. Why do you need to brainstorm when you have already analyzed it and highlighted/underlined/sticky noted your three supporting pieces of textual evidence?

1. Because we both know you haven't already done that.
2. Fun brain fact! The act of physically writing down notes, such as a brainstorm, helps to convert the information into long-term memory. Once it is converted into long-term memory, that's when you have essentially "learned" it and are no longer just holding on to the information for immediate recall just to be discarded later. Why? Because when you write things down, like a brainstorm, it is causing you to use parts of the brain that are on opposite hemispheres. It is the crossing of the hemispheres that allows the brain to retain the information and "learn" it.
3. It also provides a visual map. Since this project could take more than one sitting, it's important to have a brainstorm to refer back to in case you forget any pieces to your analysis.

Brainstorms don't have to be super detailed. In fact, the less detailed it is, the better. You just want to capture the big concepts that you plan to write about. The rest of the smaller details will come together in the outline.

There are different kinds of brainstorm maps you can try. It is best to experiment with a few until you find the one that works best for you and the way you process information. Some formats to consider are flow charts, webs, or Venn Diagrams.

For essay writing, flow charts tend to work the best. This is because the structure of the essay should flow together as one coherent idea/analysis.

What you need to include in your brainstorm are:
- What is the author's purpose/theme/thesis?
- Paraphrase or summarize your three pieces of textual evidence and include the page numbers so you can easily find them again
- Write your thesis statement for your essay

For the brainstorm you want to keep it short and sweet. It is just enough to jog your memory and provide a basic road map in case you get lost and forget where you are going.

For the author's purpose/theme/thesis, it can be a bullet point or simple statement.

For example, using "Nothing Gold Can Stay" by Robert Frost:

"Nothing Gold Can Stay" by Robert Frost

Nature's first green is gold,
Her hardest hue to hold.
Her early leaf's a flower;
But only so an hour.
Then leaf subsides to leaf.
So Eden sank to grief,
So dawn goes down to day.
Nothing gold can stay.

Theme: Everything must come to an end.

That's all you need to write down for the brainstorm. It reminds you what it is you are going to be writing about and what you need to find evidence to support.

Similarly, when you locate your three pieces of textual evidence you do not need to write down the exact quotation from the text— that comes later. You can if you want to, otherwise a page number and a quick summary of the quote is all you need.

For example:

Evidence: "Nature's green turns to gold. Line 1.""

This should be enough to trigger the memory of the passage you are looking for as well as the exact page or line in the book or poem your quotation is.

The most detailed section of your brainstorm needs to be your thesis statement. You will actually use this exact statement in your essay.

What is a thesis statement?

A thesis statement is the claim you are making for your entire critical essay.

The thesis statement will be given at the end of the introduction paragraph. It will outline your claim and the three points of evidence that you plan to use to support it.

There is a formula to follow for writing a good

thesis statement. It can be adjusted, depending on your topic or style, but for the most part this is what you are going to want to use:

"Title of work" shows (insert claim on the author's purpose/theme/thesis) through <u>point number one</u>, <u>point number two</u>, <u>point number three</u>.

The reason this formula is so successful is because it gives your essay its organization. Your thesis statement is the claim for your entire paper and it details the claims for each body paragraph. Each detailed point in your thesis gives you the exact order that your body paragraphs are going to be written in. You will start with point one for your first body paragraph, point two for your second body paragraph, and so on.

Your thesis is the most vital part of your essay and therefore is the most vital part of your brainstorm. Because of the importance of the thesis statement, you might want to brainstorm a few different ones to make sure you have the order and phrasing just right to provide the best sequence for your essay. This can include rearranging your points, or trying a few different ones to see which points best support your claim.

Let's Practice:

Below is a sample flow chart for a brainstorm. Complete the flowchart for the poem "A Book" by Emily Dickinson.

"A Book" by Emily Dickinson

He ate and drank the precious words,
His spirit grew robust;
He knew no more that he was poor,
Nor that his frame was dust.
He danced along the dingy days,
And this bequest of wings
Was but a book. What liberty
A loosened spirit brings!

Brainstorm:

Brief Summary (about):

_____

_____

_____

_____

_____

_____

Analysis (ABOUT):

Circle one that you plan to identify in your brainstorm and focus on in your essay (this is fiction so thesis will not be an option as that is for non-fiction):

Author's Purpose   Theme

Brainstorm: It's Raining Ideas!

Fill in the section below that matches your circled answer:

Author's Purpose:

_____

_____

_____

_____

_____

_____

Theme:

_____

_____

_____

_____

_____

_____

Claim (the main focus of your essay):

Textual Evidence 1 (thesis point 1):

Textual Evidence 2 (thesis point 2):

Textual Evidence 3 (thesis point 3):

Thesis Statement:

Sometimes, it is helpful to practice a few different variations of your thesis statement. Remember: the thesis statement is the basis of structure for your essay. Write it in the order you want to develop your ideas.

Thesis 2:

_____

_____

_____

_____

_____

_____

_____

_____

Thesis 3:

_____

_____

_____

_____

_____

_____

_____

_____

Now that you have your brainstorm complete, you can move on to outlining.

Chapter 3 – Line it up!

An outline is different from a brainstorm. The brainstorm is going to cover the big ideas that you need to keep track of and include in your essay, while the outline is going to break it down paragraph by paragraph.

No matter how much of an expert you become, it's best to complete both a brainstorm and an outline before writing your essay so that it is always cohesive, coherent, and concise. An outline is not the place to write a draft of your essay, it is just to make sure all the information you need is in one place.

While flow charts work best for brainstorms, bulleted lists work really well for outlines. Experiment with a few different styles if the bulleted example below doesn't work best for you. Otherwise:

Follow this outline template:

Paragraph 1: Introduction
- Hook:
- Brief summary of text and major events.
- Thesis statement:

Paragraph 2: First Body Paragraph
- Claim: the first point in your thesis
- Textual Evidence/Data: quotation
- Explanation/Warrant: explain how the quotation supports your claim.

Paragraph 3: Second Body Paragraph
- Claim: the second point in your thesis
- Textual Evidence/Data: quotation
- Explanation/Warrant: explain how the quotation supports your claim.

Paragraph 4: Third Body Paragraph
- Claim: the third point in your thesis
- Textual Evidence/ Data: quotation
- Explanation/Warrant: explain how the quotation supports your claim.

Paragraph 5: Conclusion
- Restate/paraphrase thesis:
- Summarize three body paragraph claims
- Relate it to a bigger idea to leave your reader thinking about.

You might recognize this outline as the five paragraph essay, and you're right. The five paragraph essay is a great format to use—especially for beginners. This format can be easily adjusted to add more body paragraphs if you have more than three points to discuss. You simply repeat the body paragraph format for each additional point and supporting textual evidence.

For completing the outline, you only need bullet points of information. You will tie everything together completely in the actual essay, but the outline is where you will lay it all out so you know which order your claims and evidence will appear in. This is slightly more detailed than the brainstorm, but again, the more you can simplify it the better it will be. This is mainly due to the process of writing a timed essay. You will still want an outline, but you don't want to spend more than 5 minutes on creating the outline. That way, you still have all your ideas organized but leave as much time as possible for writing your actual essay.

For example, consider this stanza from "A Poet" by Thomas Hardy:

"For loud acclaim he does not care/ By august or rich or fair,/ Nor for smart pilgrims from afar,/ Curious on where his hauntings are."

Outline: Body Paragraph 1

- **Claim:**
  The poet does not care how their work is received.
- **Textual evidence:**
  1. "For loud acclaim he does not care"
  2. "nor for smart pilgrims from afar"
- **Explanation:**
  1. Evidence 1 implies that they are not writing it for acclaim or approval by those who read it.
  2. Evidence 2 proves that the poet does not care how their work is received because they aren't looking for far off scholars to read it and analyze it.
  3. The poet does not want to hear other people's opinions and interpretations of their work.

The ideas are all there with the specific evidence, but it is only bulleted notes and not a complete paragraph. This is how the outline should look. It is more detail but not as comprehensive as the essay.

Let's Practice:

Create an outline for the body paragraphs of an essay.

"A Book" by Emily Dickinson

He ate and drank the precious words,
His spirit grew robust;
He knew no more that he was poor,
Nor that his frame was dust.
He danced along the dingy days,
And this bequest of wings
Was but a book. What liberty
A loosened spirit brings!

Thesis Statement:

_____

_____

_____

_____

_____

_____

_____

_____

First Body Paragraph

Claim (point one from thesis):

_____

_____

_____

_____

Textual Evidence (quotation):

_____

_____

_____

_____

_____

Explanation (bullet point statements):

_____

_____

_____

Second Body Paragraph

Claim (point two from thesis):

Textual Evidence (quotation):

Explanation (bullet point statements):

___

___

___

___

___

___

___

Third Body Paragraph

Claim (point three from thesis):

___

___

___

___

Textual Evidence (quotation):

Explanation (bullet point statements):

Outline: Line It Up!

You now have an outline of your body paragraphs. This should be just enough information so that you know your claim for each point from your thesis, the evidence you are using from the text, and how you plan to defend or support it. Again, your explanation should just be quick ideas that show the connection between the evidence and the claim, they do not need to be full paragraphs or complete sentences.

Next, you will work on building your introduction and conclusion paragraphs. These can be the two most difficult paragraphs because they bookend the content of your essay, but do not include any of your analysis.

Introductions

The introduction is the first paragraph of any essay. While the concept of an introduction is easy, actually writing one can be the most difficult part of your essay.

The goal of the introduction is to introduce the topic that you will be discussing to your readers, without giving too much information. You want to leave the detailed information and explanation for your body paragraphs. Just like every other part of the essay, there is a formula to writing a basic introduction.

Your introduction will start with a hook, provide a brief one to two-sentence summary of the text, and then introduce your thesis statement. Your thesis statement should be the last sentence of your introduction.

The best way to look at the introduction is that it is building background knowledge for your reader about the subject, source text, and what will be the main focus of your paper. Your introduction is leading up to your thesis statement, and subsequently your body paragraphs and analysis. There is no room for analysis in your introduction because you only want to provide analysis after your thesis statement. Once you give your thesis statement, your readers will know the focus of your paper and you can give your evidence and analysis in the following body paragraphs.

What is a hook?

The hook is the first sentence or two of your essay. It should grab the reader's attention and introduce them to the main idea you will be addressing in your essay. It is important to note, the hook is not going to be the same level of "attention grabbing" that you might expect from a fictional novel. A fictional novel wants to grab the reader's attention and pull them into a new world where they will commit to reading 300 pages. An essay doesn't require that level of commitment, so the hook will not need to be the same level of captivating. It's main purpose is to introduce the idea of what you will be talking about in an interesting way that will make the reader wonder—and continue to read—about how you are going to cover that topic.

The hook should never be a question. Starting your essay with a hypothetical question is weak and insulting to the reader. If they knew the answer, they wouldn't be reading your essay. This is why you should only provide answers and never ask questions.

For example, using "Nothing Gold Can Stay" by Robert Frost:

Theme: Everything must come to an end.

Hook: There are many wonderful sights and experiences in life, but nothing can last forever.

The hook, in this example, introduces the idea that everything must come to an end. It is the same idea that the identified theme is based on, but does not go in to as much detail as the thesis statement will. It is just a teaser of the thesis.

Let's Practice:

Write two potential hooks to introduce an essay on the poem "A Book" by Emily Dickinson.

"A Book" by Emily Dickinson

He ate and drank the precious words,
His spirit grew robust;
He knew no more that he was poor,
Nor that his frame was dust.
He danced along the dingy days,
And this bequest of wings
Was but a book. What liberty
A loosened spirit brings!

Theme:

_____

_____

_____

_____

_____

_____

_____

_____

Outline: Line It Up!

Hook 1:

_____

_____

_____

_____

_____

_____

Hook 2:

_____

_____

_____

_____

_____

_____

Again, the hook is not your thesis. It is just introducing the ideas you will be covering in your essay, but not the exact thesis statement.

After the hook in your outline for the introduction, you will make a bullet point list of three or four major events in the story. Your summary of these events will only be two sentences in the actual essay. It is just enough to provide the background information for your reader.

In an advanced format for writing a critical essay, these summary sentences will be omitted altogether. In an advanced critical essay format, you will assume the reader has read the text and does not require the summary. This is why these sentences need to be short and to the point, so that when you get to the stage where you can omit them it will not be difficult for you to do so. For now, consider these sentences to be training wheels. They are there to stabilize you until you can gain your balance, but don't get too comfortable because they will be going away.

Outline: Line It Up!

Let's Practice:

Using the poem "A Book" by Emily Dickinson, write an introduction.

"A Book" by Emily Dickinson

He ate and drank the precious words,
His spirit grew robust;
He knew no more that he was poor,
Nor that his frame was dust.
He danced along the dingy days,
And this bequest of wings
Was but a book. What liberty
A loosened spirit brings!

Hook:

_____

_____

_____

_____

_____

_____

_____

Summarize Major Events:

Thesis Statement:

Outline: Line It Up!
Put it all together:

Conclusions

Introductions and conclusions are the two hardest paragraphs to write in an essay. The introduction is difficult because you don't want to say too much too soon; the conclusion is difficult because it feels repetitive.

The nasty truth about conclusions? They should be repetitive. Your conclusion is summing up your entire paper. If the reader only read the conclusion, they should still be able to understand what your essay was about. That said, the conclusion is not just copy and paste sentences. It needs to be rephrased or restated so that it appears different.

Rephrasing your thesis will look similar to paraphrasing it. You are not going to rewrite your thesis exactly as it appeared in the introduction; instead, you are going to sum it up.

For example using "Nothing Gold Can Stay" by Robert Frost:

Thesis: The poem, "Nothing Gold Can Stay" shows the theme that everything must come to an end with the descriptions of nature's leaves, the Garden of Eden, and the progression of time.

Rephrased: The consistent imagery of life changing and fading emphasizes that nothing can last forever.

The ideas of the thesis are there, but it is different wording that summarizes what the essay explained vs. just restating it word for word.

The same method applies to summarizing the claims in your body paragraphs. After you have rephrased the thesis, you want to restate each claim from your body paragraphs but not word for word.

Conclusion: The consistent imagery of life changing and fading emphasizes that nothing can last forever. The leaves and flowers that bloom in the spring, fade to gold and then die in the winter. The Garden of Eden was once a paradise and changed to represent grief, instead. The sun rises at dawn, and progresses through day only to set showing through the steady progression of time that all of life has a cycle and everything must eventually come to an end.

Each claim from the thesis is rephrased with a paraphrased example (not a quotation,) but is nowhere near as detailed as it would be in the body paragraphs themselves.

The hardest part about the conclusion is the last sentence or two. While the first two or three sentences work to rephrase the thesis and body paragraph claims, the last sentence or two needs to relate it to a bigger idea to leave your reader thinking more about the topic. This is difficult because it can NOT be a question.

Again, you never want to ask your reader a question (rhetorical or otherwise) in your essay. They are reading your paper because they don't know the answer. Give them answers, never questions.

Since you cannot ask a question to leave your readers thinking more about, the best way to accomplish this is to connect it to an even bigger idea.

Conclusion 2: The consistent imagery of life changing and fading emphasizes that nothing can last forever. The leaves and flowers that bloom in the spring, fade to gold and then die in the winter. The Garden of Eden was once a paradise and changed to represent grief, instead. The sun rises at dawn, and progresses through day only to set showing through the steady progression of time that all of life has a cycle and everything must eventually come to an end. While the passing of life's phases and beautiful moments may cause grief, it is this natural, fleeting cycle that gives beauty to these moments. Nothing can stay forever, and that's what makes these experiences as valuable as gold.

In this example, the idea that the thesis is related to is that what makes these examples "gold" is their vulnerability to time and inability to last or "stay."

The key is that the idea has to be closely related to your thesis. You don't want to introduce an idea that is a completely different topic or belongs in its own essay. You also don't want to introduce an idea that needs to be developed and has to be explained in more than a few words. It should be obvious, but also supported by the text.

Now let's practice writing a conclusion. You will need to refer back to your outline for the three body paragraphs to complete the conclusion paragraph.

Outline: Line It Up!

Let's Practice:

Using the poem "A Book" by Emily Dickinson, write a conclusion.

"A Book" by Emily Dickinson

He ate and drank the precious words,
His spirit grew robust;
He knew no more that he was poor,
Nor that his frame was dust.
He danced along the dingy days,
And this bequest of wings
Was but a book. What liberty
A loosened spirit brings!

Rephrase your thesis:

_____

_____

_____

_____

_____

_____

_____

Rephrase claim from body paragraph 1 with example:

_____

_____

_____

_____

_____

_____

_____

_____

Rephrase claim from body paragraph 2 with example:

_____

_____

_____

_____

_____

Rephrase claim from body paragraph 3 with example:

Bigger idea to end on and wrap up with:

_____

_____

_____

_____

_____

_____

_____

_____

Put it all together:

_____

_____

_____

_____

_____

_____

_____

Outline: Line It Up!

_____

_____

_____

_____

_____

_____

_____

_____

_____

    You now have your introduction and conclusion paragraphs outlined and/or written for your essay. Now that you have your outline completed, it's time to move on to taking these pieces and fitting them together to make a cohesive essay.

Chapter 4 – Write Time, Write Place

It's the moment you've been waiting for: time to write your critical essay. At this point, you've identified your topic, brainstormed, and outlined your essay. Using all of these tools, you can finally write your essay.

When you start to write your final essay, it is important to write it in third person. This means you cannot use "I," "we," or "you." The point of a critical essay is to be objective and use evidence from the text to support your claim. To do this, you never need to refer to yourself or to the reader. You are not giving your opinion. You are not telling your reader what to think, you are simply presenting facts and analysis.

As seen in the outline, the essay has a formula and a pattern to it. Each sentence in a critical essay has a specific purpose or function.

Here is a cheat sheet to use to write your essay:

<u>Your Hook is your first sentence and it should introduce the idea you will be proving with your thesis statement and essay.</u> *Now that you've introduced the idea, introduce the text. Give a quick summary of the major events that relate to the purpose or theme you're going to be talking about.* Explicitly state what the author's purpose/theme/thesis of the text is. Thesis statement including the three points you will be discussing that prove your claim about the theme.

Your transition statement goes here, introducing your first point. <u>Make your claim for the paragraph which should be the same as your first point in your</u>

thesis statement. *Introduce your quotation or textual evidence. "Quotation and textual evidence that supports your claim goes here," (citation).* **Lead out of the quotation and transition into your explanation. Explain how your quotation supports or proves your claim. This should be a couple of sentences that explain the quotation, and how the quotation relates back to your claim.**

Transition statement into your next point. <u>Make a claim about your second point in your thesis statement.</u> *Introduce your quotation or textual evidence. "Quotation and textual evidence that supports your claim goes here," (citation).* **Lead out of the quotation and transition into your explanation. Explain how your quotation supports or proves your claim. This should be a couple of sentences that explain the quotation, and how the quotation relates back to your claim.**

Transition statement into your next point. <u>Make a claim about your third and final point in your thesis statement.</u> *Introduce your quotation or textual evidence. "Quotation and textual evidence that supports your claim goes here," (citation).* **Lead out of the quotation and transition into your explanation. Explain how your quotation supports or proves your claim. This should be a couple of sentences that explain the quotation, and how the quotation relates back to your claim.**

Restate your theme and thesis statement but make sure not to use the exact same wording. You can paraphrase yourself. <u>Give your claim and a quick example of your point in first body paragraph. Give your claim and a quick example of your point in the second body paragraph. Give your claim and a quick example</u>

<u>of your point in your third body paragraph.</u> **Wrap it up with an idea that leaves your reader with something more to think about.**

The underlined sections are going to be your claims. The italicized parts are your evidences or data. The bolded parts are your explanations.

Use this cheat sheet and you will know exactly what each sentence in your essay needs to be, what information you need to give, and in which order to give it.

In this cheat sheet, you can see how the brainstorm and outline come together to help you piece together your final essay. The brainstorm brings the big ideas, the outline gives you the smaller details and where they are going to go, and the final essay connects them all.

When writing your final essay, it is important to make sure that you cite your quotations and the text. Most critical essays will be expected to be in MLA format. In-text citations for MLA format will include the author of the text's last name and the page or line number.

Example for *Catcher in the Rye* (book):
"Quotation in my essay," (Salinger, 175).

Example for "A Poet" (poem):
"Quotation/ line of poetry" (Hardy, 12)

The reason for these citations is to avoid plagiarism and to give credit to the original author of the work that you are quoting.

It should go without saying, but: plagiarism is bad.

Stealing, replicating, and/or duplicating the original creative work of someone else without giving them credit is wrong. It is also illegal and can have serious consequences including fines and possible jail time. It's not worth it, just give the person the credit that they deserve.

Different types of texts will require different citation formats. For psychology and history papers, you will use APA formatting. For others, you may use Chicago Manual of Style. Check with your instructor before writing your essay to know which type of citation and formatting you are going to need to follow. You can also conduct a simple search online to find out.

Chapter 5 – Example Essay

It can be difficult to visualize how all the pieces fit together, so here is an original example. This essay will be written only for this book for the purposes of providing a practical application of these tools.

Master text: "A Poet" by Thomas Hardy

1. Attentive eyes, fantastic heed,
2. Assessing minds, he does not need,
3. Nor urgent writs to sup or dine,
4. Nor pledges in the roseate wine.

5. For loud acclaim he does not care
6. By the august or rich or fair,
7. Nor for smart pilgrims from afar,
8. Curious on where his hauntings are.

9. But soon or later, when you hear
10. That he has doffed this wrinkled gear,
11. Some evening, at the first star-ray,
12. Come to his graveside, pause and say:

13. "Whatever the message his to tell,
14. Two bright-souled women loved him well."
15. Stand and say that amid the dim:
16. It will be praise enough for him.

Brainstorm:

About: a poet who doesn't care what anyone thinks as long as he has the love and support of his wife and mother.

ABOUT: the people we love matter most, not the opinions of strangers or critics.

Theme: The greatest success a person can achieve is love, not critical acclaim.

Evidence: Assessing minds he doesn't need, line 2
for loud acclaim he does not care, line 5
Two women loved him, line 14
it will be enough praise, line 16

Thesis: "A Poet" challenges what it means to be successful through the poet's rejection of interpretations of his work, his uncaring for acclaim, and that he finds love to be his greatest accomplishment.

Outline:

Hook: The quest to be successful is a lifelong goal filled with hard work and determination.

Summarize Major Events: A poet writes but doesn't care about toasts, acclaim, or interpretation of his work. He doesn't care about scholars and how his work is received. What matters most to him is that someone can say, after he has passed, that he was loved by two women and that is all he wants.

Example Essay

Thesis: *A Poet* challenges what it means to be successful through the poet's rejection of interpretations of his work, his uncaring for acclaim, and that he finds love to be his greatest accomplishment.

Claim: the poet rejects interpretations of his work

Evidence/Data: "Assessing minds, he does not need," line 2

Claim: Doesn't care for acclaim or reward

Evidence/Data: "For loud acclaim he does not care," line 5
"Nor for smart pilgrims from afar,/ Curious on where his hauntings are," Line 7 and 8

Claim: Love is his greatest accomplishment

Evidence/Data: "Whatever the message his to tell,/ Two bright-souled women loved him well," lines 13-14
"It will be praise enough for him," line 16

Melissa Koons

Final Essay:

    The quest to be successful is a lifelong goal filled with hard work and determination. What it means to achieve success can vary from person to person, but Thomas Hardy poses in his poem, "A Poet," that the greatest success is to be loved. The poet in the poem doesn't care about critical acclaim or about how his work is received. The poet hopes that, upon his death, it can be said that he was loved by two women and that will be good enough for him. *A Poet* challenges what it means to be successful through the poet's rejection of interpretations of his work, his uncaring for acclaim, and that he finds love to be his greatest accomplishment.

    Most writers or artists seek reviews of their work, but the poet in "A Poet" rejects scholars' or readers' interpretations of his. The poem states that, "assessing minds, he does not need," (Hardy, line 2). Assessing minds alludes to readers and scholars who try to find meaning within the poet's words and assign value and importance to those words through analysis. Not only does the poet reject critical interpretations, but also general feedback on the quality. "Assessing minds," can also refer to readers who are evaluating how good the poet's work is. The poet "does not need" this assessment, because it is not of value to him.

    Along with interpretations of his work, the poet also rejects acclaim and praise for it. Many writers would be honored to be celebrated with "urgent writs to sup or dine" them (Hardy, line 3). This poet not only doesn't want to be celebrated, he wants no approval at all: "for loud acclaim he does not care," (Hardy, line 5). It doesn't matter to the poet if this acclaim comes from scholars or "smart pilgrims from afar,/ Curious on where his hauntings are." (Hardy, line 7-8). The poet doesn't write for other writers or to be celebrated, therefore the poet does not find those to be measures of success. Even if other writers and scholars study and try to understand the poet as a writer, the poet is unmoved by this.

The only accomplishment that the poet finds worth his life's work is love. After the poet has passed, he hopes someone can speak about him that "whatever the message his to tell,/ Two bright-souled women loved him well," (Hardy, lines 13-14). The two bright souled women can be interpreted to be the poet's mother and wife, respectively. Only their love and admiration is what the poet finds equal to success. For someone to be able to comment about the women's love of the poet, "it will be praise enough for him," (Hardy, line 16). This is because the poet values spending his life working hard for the love and appreciation of these women in his life, and his writing came second to that achievement.

The poet doesn't value critical interpretation or acclaim for his writing; what he values most is his loved ones. The poet does not need interpretation: neither critiques of meaning nor the quality of his work. The poet rejects acclaim and celebration of his skill because it is not of value to him. What the poet finds to be his greatest achievement, and for which he hopes to earn praise, is the love of the two most important women in his life. Many people equate success to a career, but success can also apply to the relationships a person builds. Both take a lifetime of work and determination, but at the end of the day one may hold a higher value than the other.

Let's Practice!

Now that you have read an example on how the whole process should come together to help you write your critical essay, it's your turn to write your own essay.

Use the poem below by Emily Bronte and create a brainstorm, an outline, and then write your essay. You can refer back to the other practice exercises that you did earlier in the book to help you.

Master Text: "Love and Friendship" by Emily Bronte

1. Love is like the wild rose-briar,
2. Friendship like the holly-tree,
3. The holly is dark when the rose-briar blooms
4. But which will bloom most constantly?
5. The wild-rose briar is sweet in the spring,
6. Its summer blossoms scent the air;
7. Yet wait till winter comes again
8. And who will call the wild-briar fair?
9. Then scorn the silly rose-wreath now
10. And deck thee with the holly's sheen,
11. That when December blights thy brow
12. He may still leave thy garland green.

Example Essay

Brainstorm:

About:

ABOUT:

Choose either Theme or Author's Purpose for your essay.

Theme:

_____

_____

_____

_____

_____

_____

_____

Author's Purpose:

_____

_____

_____

_____

_____

_____

Example Essay

Thesis Statement:

_____

_____

_____

_____

_____

_____

_____

Outline:

Hook:

_____

_____

_____

_____

_____

Summarize Major Events:

Thesis Statement:

Example Essay

Claim (point one from thesis):

_____

_____

_____

_____

Textual Evidence (quotation):

_____

_____

_____

_____

_____

Claim (point two from thesis):

_____

_____

_____

_____

Textual Evidence (quotation):

_____

_____

_____

_____

_____

_____

Claim (point three from thesis):

_____

_____

_____

_____

Textual Evidence (quotation):

_____

_____

_____

Example Essay

Rephrase your thesis:

Rephrase claim from body paragraph 1 with example:

_____

_____

_____

_____

_____

_____

_____

_____

Rephrase claim from body paragraph 2 with example:

_____

_____

_____

_____

_____

Example Essay

_____

_____

_____

_____

Rephrase claim from body paragraph 3 with example:

_____

_____

_____

_____

_____

_____

_____

_____

Bigger idea to end on and wrap up with:

Final Essay:

Example Essay

Example Essay

Example Essay

Conclusion

When you are first starting out as an essay writer, it can feel like you're wandering down a dark path without a map or a flashlight to show you the way. Learning the structure of a critical essay, as well as the purpose, provides the map and light you need to navigate through the process.

It will take time and practice to become comfortable with writing a critical essay. Following these rules and procedures will make it easier, but it will still take time before you can become an advanced essay writer. Continuing to practice each of these steps will help you learn and remember how to write a critical essay until you can do it with little effort.

With enough practice, all three of these steps can be completed in about two hours or less. This is important to note because that is typically the amount of time that is allowed on a timed exam where writing this type of essay may be required. Once you get comfortable with this style of writing an essay, you won't need to worry about compromising your planning stages in order to have enough time to write. With a solid brainstorm and outline, your essay is almost completely written. With a solid brainstorm and outline, writing your final essay will take a fraction of the time it otherwise would take to write without planning first.

The formula presented in this introductory guide is the basic foundation you need for writing a critical analysis or essay anywhere. Now that you know this formula, you can apply it whenever you need to write an analysis or critique of information. You can work toward learning more advanced critical essay techniques, but this basic formula will be sufficient for most critical essay requirements.

Now that you know the formula, you don't need to fear writing anymore. You can now write a critical essay in no time!

About the Author

Melissa Koons

Melissa Koons has always had a passion for books and creative writing. It may have started with Berenstain Bears by Stan and Jan Berenstain, but it didn't take long for authors like Lucy Culliford Babbit, Tolkien, and Robert Jordan to follow. From a young age she knew she wanted to share her love for stories with the world. She has written and published one novel, multiple short stories, and poetry. She has a BA in English and Secondary Education from the University of Northern Colorado. A former middle and high school English teacher, she now devotes her career to publishing, editing, writing, and tutoring hoping to inspire and help writers everywhere achieve their goals. When she's not working, she's taking care of her two turtles and catching up on the latest comic book franchise.

For updates, sigh up for Spine Press + Post's newsletter at their website spinepressandpost.com
Or check out Melissa's website at writeillusion.com for recent updates.
Follow Melissa on social media platforms for additional content. Facebook @authormelissakoons
or Twitter/Instagram @write_koons

Publications Director at Spine Press + Post Publishing Services

Check Out More Workbooks Coming Soon from Write Illusion and Spine Press + Post

MASTER THE ESSAY SERIES

COMPLETE INTRODUCTORY
ESSAY GUIDES AND WORKBOOKS FOR BEGINNER STUDENTS

Melissa Koons

For Author Publishing and Marketing Services

GIVE YOUR BOOK THE BACKBONE IT DESERVES.

Spine Press + Post

COMPLETE PUBLISHING & MARKETING SERVICES FOR AUTHORS & PUBLISHERS.

GET YOUR CUSTOMIZED SOLUTION AT SPINEPRESSANDPOST.COM

Melissa Koons

For More Workbooks, Check Out Porcelain Prompts Writing Prompts from Spine Press + Post

WHO WOULD'VE THOUGHT LITERATURE & LATRINES MADE SUCH A GOOD PAIR?

KEEP THESE TWO TOGETHER

PORCELAINPROMPTS.COM

MORE PROMPTS ARE RELEASED ALL THE TIME!

Printed in Great Britain
by Amazon